Twelfth Night

By William Shakespeare

Abridged for Schools and Performance

by KJ O'Hara

ISBN: 978-1530247127
Published by Antic Mind
All Enquiries to publisher@anticmind.com

ANTIC MIND

Contents

Forward

In abridging Twelfth Night for schools and performance I have brought together my experience as former Artistic Director of Antic Mind Theatre Company and of being an English and drama teacher for over 20 years.

The aim was to produce a shortened version which would improve the accessibility of the play to a younger audience and, at the same time, thoroughly engage them in this heart-warming and funny plot. In doing so, I have ensured that the essential elements of the play remain fully intact: the plot is coherent, characters are developed and all the text is original. In that sense it still contains everything an English teacher would want to see in an abridged version: key speeches and parts of scenes that teachers would want to focus on in lessons have been left alone and I've not cut anything which I thought would be useful for studying the underlying themes in the play.

The abridgement didn't require any scenes to be removed in their entirety; the main revisions have been to cut extraneous dialogue from scenes. This was done partially to allow the play to be performed by a small cast and partially to make it more streamlined and, therefore, easier for a young audience to understand and follow.

As a drama teacher, I have used this version of the text many times with my students. Sometimes we have used it for exploration, at others it has been used as a script for performance. I have even used it as the basis to make even shorter abridgements for students to perform in small groups as examination pieces.

This version allows drama teachers the flexibility to perform the play with a large or small number of students.

KJ O'Hara

Dramatis Personae

ORSINO	Duke of Illyria
SEBASTIAN	Brother to Viola
ANTONIO	a Sea Captain, Friend to Sebastian
A Sea Captain	Friend to Viola
VALENTINE and CURIO	Gentlemen attending on the Duke
SIR TOBY BELCH	Uncle to Olivia
SIR ANDREW AGUECHEEK	Suitor to Olivia
MALVOLIO	Steward to Olivia
FABIAN, FESTE	a Clown: Servants to Olivia
OLIVIA	a rich Countess
VIOLA	in love with the Duke
MARIA	Olivia's Woman

Lords, Priests, Sailors, Officers, Musicians, and other Attendants

ACT I

Act 1 Scene I

DUKE ORSINO's palace

Enter DUKE ORSINO, CURIO, and other Lords; Musicians attending

DUKE ORSINO

If music be the food of love, play on;
Give me excess of it, that, surfeiting,
The appetite may sicken, and so die.
O, when mine eyes did see Olivia first,
That instant was I turn'd into a hart;
And my desires, like fell and cruel hounds,
E'er since pursue me.

Enter VALENTINE

How now! what news from her?

VALENTINE

So please my lord, I might not be admitted;
But from her handmaid do return this answer:
The element itself, till seven years' heat,
Shall not behold her face at ample view;
All this to season a brother's dead love,
Which she would keep fresh
And lasting in her sad remembrance.

DUKE ORSINO

How will she love, when the rich golden shaft
Hath kill'd the flock of all affections else
That live in her; when liver, brain and heart,
These sovereign thrones, are all supplied, and fill'd
Her sweet perfections with one self king!

Exeunt

Act I Scene II

The sea-coast

Enter VIOLA, a Captain, and Sailors

VIOLA What country, friends, is this?

Captain This is Illyria, lady.

VIOLA And what should I do in Illyria?
My brother perchance he is not drown'd:
What think you, sailors?

Captain True, madam: after our ship did split,
I saw your brother bind himself,
To a strong mast that lived upon the sea;

VIOLA For saying so, there's gold:
Know'st thou this country?

Captain Ay, madam, well.

VIOLA Who governs here?

Captain A noble duke, in nature as in name.

VIOLA What is the name?

Captain Orsino.

VIOLA Orsino! I have heard my father name him:
He was a bachelor then.

Captain And so is now, or was so very late;
For but a month 'twas fresh in murmur,
That he did seek the love of fair Olivia.
A virtuous maid, the daughter of a count
That died some twelvemonth since, then leaving her
In the protection of his son, her brother,

Who shortly also died: for whose dear love,
They say, she hath abjured the company
And sight of men.

VIOLA

O that I served that lady.

Captain

That were hard to compass;
Because she will admit no kind of suit,
No, not the duke's.

VIOLA

There is a fair behaviour in thee, captain;
I prithee, and I'll pay thee bounteously,
Conceal me what I am, and be my aid
For such disguise as haply shall become
The form of my intent. I'll serve this duke.

Exeunt

Act I Scene III

OLIVIA'S house

Enter SIR TOBY BELCH and MARIA

SIR TOBY BELCH   What a plague means my niece, to take the death of
her brother thus? I am sure care's an enemy to life.

MARIA   By my troth, Sir Toby, you must come in earlier o'
nights: your cousin, my lady, takes great
exceptions to your ill hours.
That quaffing and drinking will undo you: I heard
my lady talk of it yesterday; and of a foolish
knight that you brought in one night here to be her
wooer.

SIR TOBY BELCH   Who, Sir Andrew Aguecheek?

MARIA   Ay, he.

SIR TOBY BELCH   He's as tall a man as any's in Illyria.
Why, he has three thousand ducats a year.
He speaks three or four languages
and hath all the good gifts of nature.

MARIA   Besides that he's a fool, he's a great quarreller:
And but that he hath the gift of a coward to allay the gust
He hath in quarrelling, 'tis thought he would quickly
Have the gift of a grave. Fare you well.

Exit

Enter Sir Andrew

SIR ANDREW   Faith, I'll home to-morrow, Sir Toby: your niece
will not be seen; or if she be, it's four to one
she'll none of me: the count himself here hard by woos
her.

SIR TOBY BELCH   She'll none o' the count: she'll not match above
                        her degree, neither in estate, years, nor wit; I
                        have heard her swear't. Tut, there's life in't,
                        man.

SIR ANDREW   I'll stay a month longer.
Exeunt

Act I Scene IV

DUKE ORSINO's palace

Enter VALENTINE and VIOLA in man's attire

VALENTINE	If the duke continue these favours towards you, Cesario, you are like to be much advanced: he hath known you but three days, and already you are no stranger.
VIOLA	I thank you. Here comes the count.

Enter DUKE ORSINO, CURIO, and Attendants

DUKE ORSINO	Who saw Cesario, ho?
VIOLA	On your attendance, my lord; here.
DUKE ORSINO	Cesario, I have unclasp'd to thee The book even of my secret soul: Therefore, good youth, address thy gait unto her; Be not denied access, stand at her doors, And tell them, there thy fixed foot shall grow Till thou have audience.
VIOLA	Say I do speak with her, my lord, what then?
DUKE ORSINO	O, then unfold the passion of my love, Surprise her with discourse of my dear faith: It shall become thee well to act my woes. Prosper well in this, And thou shalt live as freely as thy lord, To call his fortunes thine.
VIOLA	I'll do my best To woo your lady: *[Aside]* yet, a barful strife! Whoe'er I woo, myself would be his wife.

Exeunt

Act I Scene V

OLIVIA'S house.

Enter Olivia and Malvolio

MALVOLIO   Madam, there is at the gate a young fellow
Swears he will speak with you.
I told him you were sick; he takes on him to
understand so much, and therefore comes to speak
with you. I told him you were asleep; he seems to
have a foreknowledge of that too, and therefore
comes to speak with you. What is to be said to him,
lady? he's fortified against any denial.

OLIVIA   Tell him he shall not speak with me.

MALVOLIO   Has been told so; and he says, he'll stand at your
door like a sheriff's post, and be the supporter to
a bench, but he'll speak with you.

OLIVIA   What kind o' man is he?

MALVOLIO   Why, of mankind.

OLIVIA   What manner of man?

MALVOLIO   Of very ill manner; he'll speak with you, will you or no.

OLIVIA   Of what personage and years is he?

MALVOLIO   Not yet old enough for a man, nor young enough for
a boy. He is very well-favoured and he speaks very
shrewishly; one would think his mother's milk were
scarce out of him.

OLIVIA   Let him approach: call in my gentlewoman.

MALVOLIO   Gentlewoman, my lady calls.

Exit
Enter MARIA

OLIVIA   Give me my veil: come, throw it o'er my face.
                     We'll once more hear Orsino's embassy.

Enter VIOLA, and Attendants

VIOLA   The honourable lady of the house, which is she?

OLIVIA   Speak to me; I shall answer for her.
                     Your will?

VIOLA   Most radiant, exquisite and unmatchable beauty,--I
                     pray you, tell me if this be the lady of the house,
                     for I never saw her: I would be loath to cast away
                     my speech, for besides that it is excellently well
                     penned, I have taken great pains to con it.

OLIVIA   Whence came you, sir?

VIOLA   I can say little more than I have studied, and that
                     question's out of my part. Are you the lady of the house?

OLIVIA   If I do not usurp myself, I am. Speak your office.

VIOLA   It alone concerns your ear.

OLIVIA   Give us the place alone: we will hear this divinity.

Exeunt MARIA and Attendants

                     Now, sir, what is your text?

VIOLA   Most sweet lady,--

OLIVIA   A comfortable doctrine, and much may be said of it.
                     Where lies your text?

VIOLA   In Orsino's bosom.

OLIVIA	In his bosom! In what chapter of his bosom?
VIOLA	To answer by the method, in the first of his heart.
OLIVIA	O, I have read it: it is heresy. Have you no more to say?
VIOLA	Good madam, let me see your face.
OLIVIA	Have you any commission from your lord to negotiate with my face? You are now out of your text: but we will draw the curtain and show you the picture. Look you, sir, is't not well done?

Unveiling

VIOLA	Excellently done, if God did all.
	'Tis beauty truly blent, whose red and white
	Nature's own sweet and cunning hand laid on:
OLIVIA	Were you sent hither to praise me?
VIOLA	I see you what you are, you are too proud;
	But, if you were the devil, you are fair.
	My lord and master loves you: O, such love
	Could be but recompensed, though you were crown'd
	The nonpareil of beauty!
OLIVIA	How does he love me?
VIOLA	With adorations, fertile tears,
	With groans that thunder love, with sighs of fire.
OLIVIA	Your lord does know my mind;
	I suppose him virtuous, know him noble,
	Of great estate, and a gracious person:
	but yet I cannot love him.
	He might have took his answer long ago.
VIOLA	If I did love you in my master's flame,
	With such a suffering, such a deadly life,

	In your denial I would find no sense; I would not understand it.
OLIVIA	Why, what would you?

VIOLA	Make me a willow cabin at your gate, And call upon my soul within the house; Halloo your name to the reverberate hills And make the babbling gossip of the air Cry out 'Olivia!' O, You should not rest But you should pity me!

OLIVIA	You might do much. What is your parentage?

VIOLA	Above my fortunes, yet my state is well: I am a gentleman.

OLIVIA	Get you to your lord; I cannot love him: let him send no more; Unless, perchance, you come to me again, To tell me how he takes it. Fare you well: I thank you for your pains: spend this for me.

VIOLA	I am no fee'd post, lady; keep your purse: My master, not myself, lacks recompense. Love make his heart of flint that you shall love; And let your fervour, like my master's, be Placed in contempt! Farewell, fair cruelty.

Exit

OLIVIA	'What is your parentage?' 'Above my fortunes, yet my state is well: I am a gentleman.' I'll be sworn thou art; Thy tongue, thy face, thy limbs, actions and spirit, Do give thee five-fold blazon: not too fast: soft, soft! Unless the master were the man. How now! Even so quickly may one catch the plague? Methinks I feel this youth's perfections With an invisible and subtle stealth

To creep in at mine eyes. Well, let it be.
What ho, Malvolio!

Re-enter MALVOLIO

MALVOLIO   Here, madam, at your service.

OLIVIA   Run after that same peevish messenger,
The county's man: he left this ring behind him,
Would I or not: tell him I'll none of it.
Desire him not to flatter with his lord,
Nor hold him up with hopes; I am not for him:
If that the youth will come this way to-morrow,
I'll give him reasons for't: hie thee, Malvolio.

MALVOLIO   Madam, I will.
Exit

OLIVIA   I do I know not what, and fear to find
Mine eye too great a flatterer for my mind.
Fate, show thy force: ourselves we do not owe;
What is decreed must be, and be this so.

Exit

ACT II

Act II Scene I

The sea-coast

Enter ANTONIO and SEBASTIAN

ANTONIO   Will you stay no longer? nor will you not that I go with you?

SEBASTIAN   By your patience, no. My stars shine darkly over me: I shall crave of you your leave that I may bear my evils alone: it were a bad recompense for your love, to lay any of them on you.

ANTONIO   Let me yet know of you whither you are bound.

SEBASTIAN   No, sooth, sir: but you must know my name is Sebastian. My father was Sebastian of Messaline. He left behind him myself and a sister, both born in an hour: if the heavens had been pleased, would we had so ended! but you, sir, altered that; for some hour before you took me from the breach of the sea was my sister drowned.

ANTONIO   Alas the day!

SEBASTIAN   A lady, sir, though it was said she much resembled me, was yet of many accounted beautiful: she bore a mind that envy could not but call fair. Fare ye well at once: I am bound to the Count Orsino's court.

Exit

ANTONIO   The gentleness of all the gods go with thee! I have many enemies in Orsino's court, Else would I very shortly see thee there.

But, come what may, I do adore thee so,
That danger shall seem sport, and I will go.

Exit

Act II Scene II

A street

Enter VIOLA, MALVOLIO following

MALVOLIO   Were not you even now with the Countess Olivia?

VIOLA   Even now, sir; on a moderate pace I have since
arrived but hither.

MALVOLIO   She returns this ring to you, sir: you might have
saved me my pains, to have taken it away yourself.
She adds, moreover, that you should put your lord
into a desperate assurance she will none of him:
and one thing more, that you be never so hardy to
come again in his affairs, unless it be to report
your lord's taking of this. Receive it so.

VIOLA   She took the ring of me: I'll none of it.

MALVOLIO   Come, sir, you peevishly threw it to her; and her
will is, it should be so returned: if it be worth
stooping for, there it lies in your eye; if not, be
it his that finds it.

Exit

VIOLA   I left no ring with her: what means this lady?
Fortune forbid my outside have not charm'd her!
She loves me; poor lady, she were better love a dream.
Disguise, I see, thou art a wickedness,
Wherein the pregnant enemy does much.
How will this fadge? my master loves her dearly;
And I, poor monster, fond as much on him;
And she, mistaken, seems to dote on me.
What will become of this?
O time! thou must untangle this, not I;
It is too hard a knot for me to untie!

Exit

Act III Scene III

OLIVIA's house

Enter SIR TOBY BELCH and SIR ANDREW and CLOWN

SIR TOBY BELCH   Come on; there is sixpence for you: let's have a song.

Clown   Would you have a love-song, or a song of good life?

SIR TOBY BELCH   A love-song, a love-song.

SIR ANDREW   Ay, ay: I care not for good life.

Clown   [Sings]   O mistress mine, where are you roaming?
O, stay and hear; your true love's coming,
That can sing both high and low:
Trip no further, pretty sweeting;
Journeys end in lovers meeting,
Every wise man's son doth know.

Enter MARIA

MARIA   What a caterwauling do you keep here! If my lady
have not called up her steward Malvolio and bid him
turn you out of doors, never trust me.

SIR TOBY BELCH   [Sings] 'O, the twelfth day of December,'--

MARIA   For the love o' God, peace!

Enter MALVOLIO

MALVOLIO   My masters, are you mad? Have ye
no wit, manners, nor honesty, but to gabble like
tinkers at this time of night? Do ye make an
alehouse of my lady's house? Is there no respect
of place, persons, nor time in you?

SIR TOBY BELCH   We did keep time, sir, in our catches. Sneck up!

MALVOLIO   Sir Toby, I must be round with you. My lady bade me
tell you, that, though she harbours you as her
kinsman, she's nothing allied to your disorders. If
you can separate yourself and your misdemeanors, you
are welcome to the house; if not, an it would please
you to take leave of her, she is very willing to bid
you farewell.

SIR TOBY BELCH   Out o' tune, sir: ye lie. Art any more than a
steward? Dost thou think, because thou art
virtuous, there shall be no more cakes and ale?
Go, sir, rub your chain with crumbs.
A stoup of wine, Maria!

MALVOLIO   Mistress Mary, if you prized my lady's favour at any
thing more than contempt, you would not give means
for this uncivil rule: she shall know of it, by this hand.

Exit

MARIA   Go shake your ears.

SIR ANDREW   'Twere as good a deed as to drink when a man's
a-hungry, to challenge him the field, and then to
break promise with him and make a fool of him.

SIR TOBY BELCH   Do't, knight: I'll write thee a challenge: or I'll
deliver thy indignation to him by word of mouth.

MARIA   Sweet Sir Toby, be patient for tonight: since the
youth of the count's was today with thy lady, she is
much out of quiet. For Monsieur Malvolio, let me
alone with him: if I do not gull him into a
nayword, and make him a common recreation, do not
think I have wit enough to lie straight in my bed:
I know I can do it.

SIR TOBY BELCH   Possess us, possess us; tell us something of him.

MARIA	Marry, sir, sometimes he is a kind of puritan.
SIR ANDREW	O, if I thought that I'ld beat him like a dog!
MARIA	The devil a puritan that he is; an affectioned ass, that it is his grounds of faith that all that look on him love him; and on that vice in him will my revenge find notable cause to work.
SIR TOBY BELCH	What wilt thou do?
MARIA	I will drop in his way some obscure epistles of love; wherein, by the colour of his beard, the shape of his leg, the manner of his gait, the expressure of his eye, forehead, and complexion, he shall find himself most feelingly personated. I can write very like my lady your niece.
SIR TOBY BELCH	Excellent! I smell a device.
SIR ANDREW	I have't in my nose too.
SIR TOBY BELCH	He shall think, by the letters that thou wilt drop, that they come from my niece, and that she's in love with him.
MARIA	My purpose is, indeed, a horse of that colour.
SIR ANDREW	And your horse now would make him an ass.
MARIA	Ass, I doubt not.
SIR ANDREW	O, 'twill be admirable!
MARIA	Sport royal, I warrant you: I know my physic will work with him. I will plant you two, and let the fool make a third, where he shall find the letter: observe his construction of it. For this night, to bed, and dream on the event. Farewell.

Exeunt

Act II Scene IV

DUKE ORSINO's palace

Enter DUKE ORSINO, VIOLA, CURIO, and others

DUKE ORSINO   Give me some music. Now, good morrow, friends.
Now, good Cesario, how dost thou like this tune?

VIOLA   It gives a very echo to the seat
Where Love is throned.

DUKE ORSINO   Thou dost speak masterly:
My life upon't, young though thou art, thine eye
Hath stay'd upon some favour that it loves:
Hath it not, boy?

VIOLA   A little, by your favour.

DUKE ORSINO   What kind of woman is't?

VIOLA   Of your complexion.

DUKE ORSINO   She is not worth thee, then. What years, i' faith?

VIOLA   About your years, my lord.

DUKE ORSINO   Too old by heaven: let thy love be younger than thyself,
Or thy affection cannot hold the bent;
For women are as roses, whose fair flower
Being once display'd, doth fall that very hour.

VIOLA   And so they are: alas, that they are so;
To die, even when they to perfection grow!

DUKE ORSINO   Once more, Cesario,
Get thee to yond same sovereign cruelty:
Tell her, my love, more noble than the world,
Prizes not quantity of dirty lands;
The parts that fortune hath bestow'd upon her,

Tell her, I hold as giddily as fortune;
But 'tis that miracle and queen of gems
That nature pranks her in attracts my soul.

VIOLA

But if she cannot love you, sir?

DUKE ORSINO

I cannot be so answer'd.

VIOLA

Sooth, but you must.
Say that some lady, as perhaps there is,
Hath for your love a great a pang of heart
As you have for Olivia: you cannot love her;
You tell her so; must she not then be answer'd?

DUKE ORSINO

There is no woman's sides
Can bide the beating of so strong a passion
As love doth give my heart; make no compare
Between that love a woman can bear me
And that I owe Olivia.

VIOLA

Ay, but I know--

DUKE ORSINO

What dost thou know?

VIOLA

Too well what love women to men may owe:
In faith, they are as true of heart as we.
My father had a daughter loved a man,
As it might be, perhaps, were I a woman,
I should your lordship.

DUKE ORSINO

And what's her history?

VIOLA

A blank, my lord. She never told her love,
But let concealment, like a worm i' the bud,
Feed on her damask cheek: she pined in thought,
And with a green and yellow melancholy
She sat like patience on a monument,
Smiling at grief. Was not this love indeed?
We men may say more, swear more: but indeed

Our shows are more than will; for still we prove
Much in our vows, but little in our love.

DUKE ORSINO   But died thy sister of her love, my boy?

VIOLA   I am all the daughters of my father's house,
And all the brothers too: and yet I know not.
Sir, shall I to this lady?

DUKE ORSINO   Ay, that's the theme.
To her in haste; give her this jewel; say,
My love can give no place, bide no denay.

Exeunt

Act II Scene V

OLIVIA's garden

Enter SIR TOBY BELCH, SIR ANDREW, and FABIAN

SIR TOBY BELCH   Come thy ways, Signior Fabian.

FABIAN   Nay, I'll come: if I lose a scruple of this sport,
let me be boiled to death with melancholy.

SIR TOBY BELCH   Wouldst thou not be glad to have the niggardly
rascally sheep-biter come by some notable shame?

FABIAN   I would exult, man: you know, he brought me out o'
favour with my lady about a bear-baiting here.

SIR TOBY BELCH   To anger him we'll have the bear again; and we will
fool him black and blue: shall we not, Sir Andrew?

SIR ANDREW   An we do not, it is pity of our lives.

SIR TOBY BELCH   Here comes the little villain.

Enter MARIA

How now, my metal of India!

MARIA   Get ye all three into the box-tree: Malvolio's
coming down this walk: he has been yonder i' the
sun practising behaviour to his own shadow this half
hour: observe him, for the love of mockery; for I
know this letter will make a contemplative idiot of
him. Close, in the name of jesting! Lie thou there,
[Throws down a letter] for here comes the trout that must
be caught with tickling.

Exit

Enter MALVOLIO

MALVOLIO	*[Taking up the letter]* What employment have we here?
FABIAN	Now is the woodcock near the gin.
SIR TOBY BELCH	O, peace! and the spirit of humour intimate reading aloud to him!
MALVOLIO	By my life, this is my lady's hand these be her very C's, her U's and her T's and thus makes she her great P's. It is, in contempt of question, her hand. [Reads] 'To the unknown beloved, this, and my good wishes:'--her very phrases! 'tis my lady. To whom should this be?
FABIAN	This wins him, liver and all.
MALVOLIO	[Reads] Jove knows I love: But who? Lips, do not move; No man must know. 'No man must know.' What follows? the numbers altered! 'No man must know:' if this should be thee, Malvolio?
SIR TOBY BELCH	Marry, hang thee, brock!
MALVOLIO	[Reads] I may command where I adore; But silence, like a Lucrece knife, With bloodless stroke my heart doth gore: M, O, A, I, doth sway my life.
FABIAN	A fustian riddle!
SIR TOBY BELCH	Excellent wench, say I.
MALVOLIO	'M, O, A, I, doth sway my life.' Nay, but first, let me see, let me see, let me see. 'I may command where I adore.' Why, she may command me: I serve her; she is my lady. and the end, --what should that alphabetical position portend? If I could make that resemble something in me,

--Softly! M, O, A,I,--

SIR TOBY BELCH O, ay, make up that: he is now at a cold scent.

MALVOLIO M, O, A, I; every one of these letters are in my name.
Soft! here follows prose.
[Reads] 'If this fall into thy hand, revolve. In my stars I
am above thee; but be not afraid of greatness: some
are born great, some achieve greatness, and some
have greatness thrust upon 'em. Thy Fates open
their hands; let thy blood and spirit embrace them;
and, to inure thyself to what thou art like to be,
cast thy humble slough and appear fresh.
She thus advises thee that sighs for thee.
Remember who commended thy
yellow stockings, and wished to see thee ever
cross-gartered: I say, remember. Go to, thou art
made, if thou desirest to be so; if not, let me see
thee a steward still, the fellow of servants, and
not worthy to touch Fortune's fingers. Farewell.
She that would alter services with thee,
THE FORTUNATE-UNHAPPY.'
Daylight and champaign discovers not more:
I do not now fool myself, to let imagination jade
me; for every reason excites to this, that my lady
loves me. She did commend my yellow stockings of
late, she did praise my leg being cross-gartered;
and in this she manifests herself to my love, and
with a kind of injunction drives me to these habits
of her liking. I thank my stars I am happy. I will
be strange, stout, in yellow stockings, and
cross-gartered, even with the swiftness of putting
on. Jove and my stars be praised! Here is yet a
postscript. *[Reads]* 'Thou canst not choose but know who
I am. If thou entertainest my love, let it appear in thy
smiling; thy smiles become thee well; therefore in my
presence still smile, dear my sweet, I prithee.'
Jove, I thank thee: I will smile; I will do
everything that thou wilt have me.

Exit

SIR TOBY BELCH	I could marry this wench for this device.
SIR ANDREW	So could I too.

FABIAN	Here comes my noble gull-catcher.

Re-enter MARIA

SIR TOBY BELCH	Why, thou hast put him in such a dream, that when the image of it leaves him he must run mad.

MARIA	Nay, but say true; does it work upon him?

SIR TOBY BELCH	Like aqua-vitae with a midwife.

MARIA	If you will then see the fruits of the sport, mark his first approach before my lady: he will come to her in yellow stockings, and 'tis a colour she abhors, and cross-gartered, a fashion she detests; and he will smile upon her, which will now be so unsuitable to her disposition, being addicted to a melancholy as she is, that it cannot but turn him into a notable contempt. If you will see it, follow me.

Exeunt

ACT III

Act III Scene I

OLIVIA's garden

Enter VIOLA, OLIVIA and MARIA

VIOLA   Most excellent accomplished lady, the heavens rain
                 odours on you!

OLIVIA   Give me your hand, sir.

VIOLA   My duty, madam, and most humble service.

OLIVIA   What is your name?

VIOLA   Cesario is your servant's name, fair princess.

OLIVIA   My servant, sir! You're servant to the Count Orsino,
                 youth.

VIOLA   And he is yours, and his must needs be yours:
                 Your servant's servant is your servant, madam.

OLIVIA   For him, I think not on him: for his thoughts,
                 Would they were blanks, rather than fill'd with me!

VIOLA   Madam, I come to whet your gentle thoughts
                 On his behalf.

OLIVIA   O, by your leave, I pray you,
                 I bade you never speak again of him:
                 But, would you undertake another suit,
                 I had rather hear you to solicit that
                 Than music from the spheres.

VIOLA   Dear lady,--

OLIVIA	Give me leave, beseech you. I did send,
	After the last enchantment you did here,
	A ring in chase of you: so did I abuse
	Myself, my servant and, I fear me, you:
	Under your hard construction must I sit,
	To force that on you, in a shameful cunning,
	Which you knew none of yours: what might you think?
	Have you not set mine honour at the stake
	And baited it with all the unmuzzled thoughts
	That tyrannous heart can think? To one of your receiving
	Enough is shown: a cypress, not a bosom,
	Hideth my heart. So, let me hear you speak.

VIOLA	I pity you.

OLIVIA	That's a degree to love.

VIOLA	No, not a grize; for 'tis a vulgar proof,
	That very oft we pity enemies.

OLIVIA	Why, then, methinks 'tis time to smile again.
	O, world, how apt the poor are to be proud!
	If one should be a prey, how much the better
	To fall before the lion than the wolf!

Clock strikes

	The clock upbraids me with the waste of time.
	Be not afraid, good youth, I will not have you:
	And yet, when wit and youth is come to harvest,
	Your were is alike to reap a proper man:
	There lies your way, due west.

VIOLA	Then westward-ho! Grace and good disposition
	Attend your ladyship!
	You'll nothing, madam, to my lord by me?

OLIVIA	Stay: I prithee, tell me what thou thinkest of me.

VIOLA	That you do think you are not what you are.

OLIVIA	If I think so, I think the same of you.

VIOLA	Then think you right: I am not what I am.
OLIVIA	I would you were as I would have you be!
VIOLA	Would it be better, madam, than I am?
OLIVIA	O, what a deal of scorn looks beautiful In the contempt and anger of his lip! Cesario, by the roses of the spring, By maidhood, honour, truth and every thing, I love thee so, that, maugre all thy pride, Nor wit nor reason can my passion hide. Do not extort thy reasons from this clause, For that I woo, thou therefore hast no cause, But rather reason thus with reason fetter, Love sought is good, but given unsought better.
VIOLA	By innocence I swear, and by my youth I have one heart, one bosom and one truth, And that no woman has; nor never none Shall mistress be of it, save I alone. And so adieu, good madam: never more Will I my master's tears to you deplore.
OLIVIA	Yet come again; for thou perhaps mayst move That heart, which now abhors, to like his love.

Exeunt

Act III Scene II

OLIVIA's house

Enter SIR TOBY BELCH, SIR ANDREW, and FABIAN

SIR ANDREW   No, faith, I'll not stay a jot longer.

SIR TOBY BELCH   Thy reason, dear venom, give thy reason.

SIR ANDREW   Marry, I saw your niece do more favours to the
count's serving-man than ever she bestowed upon me;
I saw't i' the orchard.

FABIAN   She did show favour to the youth in your sight only
to exasperate you, to awake your dormouse valour, to
put fire in your heart and brimstone in your liver.

SIR TOBY BELCH   Why, then, build me thy fortunes upon the basis of
valour. Challenge me the count's youth to fight
with him; hurt him in eleven places: my niece shall
take note of it; and assure thyself, there is no
love-broker in the world can more prevail in man's
commendation with woman than report of valour.

FABIAN   There is no way but this, Sir Andrew.

SIR ANDREW   Will either of you bear me a challenge to him?

SIR TOBY BELCH   Go, write it in a martial hand; be curst and brief;
it is no matter how witty, so it be eloquent and fun
of invention: Let there be gall enough in thy ink,
though thou write with a goose-pen, no matter: about it.

SIR ANDREW   Where shall I find you?

SIR TOBY BELCH   We'll call thee at the cubiculo: go.

Exit SIR ANDREW

FABIAN   We shall have a rare letter from him: but you'll not deliver't?

SIR TOBY BELCH   Never trust me, then; and by all means stir on the youth to an answer. I think oxen and wainropes cannot hale them together. For Andrew, if he were opened, and you find so much blood in his liver as will clog the foot of a flea, I'll eat the rest of the anatomy.

FABIAN   And his opposite, the youth, bears in his visage no great presage of cruelty.

Enter MARIA

SIR TOBY BELCH   Look, where the youngest wren of nine comes.

MARIA   If you desire the spleen, and will laugh yourself into stitches, follow me. Yond gull Malvolio is in yellow stockings.

SIR TOBY BELCH   And cross-gartered?

MARIA   Most villainously. He does obey every point of the letter that I dropped to betray him: you have not seen such a thing as 'tis. I can hardly forbear hurling things at him. I know my lady will strike him: if she do, he'll smile and take't for a great favour.

SIR TOBY BELCH   Come, bring us, bring us where he is.
Exeunt

Act III Scene III

Enter SEBASTIAN and ANTONIO

SEBASTIAN   I would not by my will have troubled you;
But, since you make your pleasure of your pains,
I will no further chide you.

ANTONIO   I could not stay behind you: my desire,
More sharp than filed steel, did spur me forth
in your pursuit.

SEBASTIAN   My kind Antonio,
I can no other answer make but thanks.
What's to do? Shall we go see the reliques of this town?

ANTONIO   To-morrow, sir: best first go see your lodging.

SEBASTIAN   I am not weary, and 'tis long to night:
I pray you, let us satisfy our eyes
With the memorials and the things of fame
That do renown this city.

ANTONIO   Would you'ld pardon me;
I do not without danger walk these streets:
Once, in a sea-fight, 'gainst the count his galleys
I did some service; of such note indeed,
That were I ta'en here it would scarce be answer'd.

SEBASTIAN   Do not then walk too open.

ANTONIO   It doth not fit me. Hold, sir, here's my purse.
In the south suburbs, at the Elephant,
Is best to lodge: I will bespeak our diet,
Whiles you beguile the time and feed your knowledge
With viewing of the town: there shall you have me.

SEBASTIAN   Why I your purse?

ANTONIO	Haply your eye shall light upon some toy You have desire to purchase; and your store, I think, is not for idle markets, sir.
SEBASTIAN	I'll be your purse-bearer and leave you For an hour.
ANTONIO	To the Elephant.
SEBASTIAN *Exeunt*	I do remember.

Act III Scene IV

OLIVIA's garden

Enter OLIVIA and MARIA

OLIVIA
I have sent after him: he says he'll come;
How shall I feast him? what bestow of him?
For youth is bought more oft than begg'd or borrow'd.
I speak too loud.
Where is Malvolio? he is sad and civil,
And suits well for a servant with my fortunes:
Where is Malvolio?

MARIA
He's coming, madam; but in very strange manner. He
is, sure, possessed, madam.

OLIVIA
Why, what's the matter? does he rave?

MARIA
No. madam, he does nothing but smile: your
ladyship were best to have some guard about you, if
he come; for, sure, the man is tainted in's wits.

OLIVIA
Go call him hither.
Exit MARIA

I am as mad as he,
If sad and merry madness equal be.

Re-enter MARIA, with MALVOLIO

How now, Malvolio!

MALVOLIO
Sweet lady, ho, ho.

OLIVIA
Smilest thou?
I sent for thee upon a sad occasion.

MALVOLIO
Sad, lady! I could be sad: this does make some
obstruction in the blood, this cross-gartering; but

	what of that? if it please the eye of one, it is with me as the very true sonnet is, 'Please one, and please all.'
OLIVIA	Why, how dost thou, man? what is the matter with thee?
MALVOLIO	Not black in my mind, though yellow in my legs. It did come to his hands, and commands shall be executed: I think we do know the sweet Roman hand.
OLIVIA	Wilt thou go to bed, Malvolio?
MALVOLIO	To bed! ay, sweet-heart, and I'll come to thee.
OLIVIA	God comfort thee! Why dost thou smile so and kiss thy hand so oft?
MARIA	How do you, Malvolio?
MALVOLIO	At your request!
MARIA	Why appear you with this ridiculous boldness before my lady?
MALVOLIO	'Be not afraid of greatness:' 'twas well writ.
OLIVIA	What meanest thou by that, Malvolio?
MALVOLIO	'Some are born great,'--
OLIVIA	Ha!
MALVOLIO	'Some achieve greatness,'--
OLIVIA	What sayest thou?
MALVOLIO	'And some have greatness thrust upon them.'
OLIVIA	Heaven restore thee!

MALVOLIO	'Remember who commended thy yellow stocking s,'--
OLIVIA	Thy yellow stockings!
MALVOLIO	'And wished to see thee cross-gartered.'
OLIVIA	Cross-gartered!
MALVOLIO	'Go to thou art made, if thou desirest to be so;'--
OLIVIA	Am I made?
MALVOLIO	'If not, let me see thee a servant still.'
OLIVIA	Why, this is very midsummer madness.

Enter Servant

Servant	Madam, the young gentleman of the Count Orsino's is returned: I could hardly entreat him back: he attends your ladyship's pleasure.
OLIVIA	I'll come to him.

Exit Servant

Good Maria, let this fellow be looked to. Where's my cousin Toby? Let some of my people have a special care of him: I would not have him miscarry for the half of my dowry.

Exeunt OLIVIA and MARIA

MALVOLIO	O, ho! do you come near me now? no worse man than Sir Toby to look to me! This concurs directly with the letter: she sends him on purpose, that I may appear stubborn to him; for she incites me to that in the letter. 'Cast thy humble slough,' says she; 'be opposite with a kinsman, surly with servants'. I have limed her; but it is Jove's doing, and Jove make me

thankful! And when she went away now, 'Let this
fellow be looked to:' fellow! not Malvolio, nor
after my degree, but fellow. Why, every thing
adheres together. Nothing
that can be can come between me and the full
prospect of my hopes. Well, Jove, not I, is the
doer of this, and he is to be thanked.

Re-enter MARIA, with SIR TOBY BELCH and FABIAN

SIR TOBY BELCH	Which way is he, in the name of sanctity? If all the devils of hell be drawn in little, and Legion himself possessed him, yet I'll speak to him.
FABIAN	Here he is, here he is. How is't with you, sir? how is't with you, man?
MALVOLIO	Go off; I discard you: let me enjoy my private: go off.
MARIA	Lo, how hollow the fiend speaks within him! did not I tell you? Sir Toby, my lady prays you to have a care of him.
MALVOLIO	Ah, ha! does she so?
SIR TOBY BELCH	Go to, go to; peace, peace; we must deal gently with him: let me alone. How do you, Malvolio? how is't with you? What, man! defy the devil: consider, he's an enemy to mankind.
MALVOLIO	Do you know what you say?
MARIA	La you, an you speak ill of the devil, how he takes it at heart! Pray God, he be not bewitched!
MALVOLIO	How now, mistress!
MARIA	O Lord!

FABIAN	No way but gentleness; gently, gently: the fiend is rough, and will not be roughly used.
MALVOLIO	Sir!
SIR TOBY BELCH	Ay, Biddy, come with me. What, man! 'tis not for gravity to play at cherry-pit with Satan: hang him, foul collier!
MARIA	Get him to say his prayers, good Sir Toby, get him to pray.
MALVOLIO	My prayers, minx!
MARIA	No, I warrant you, he will not hear of godliness.
MALVOLIO	Go, hang yourselves all! you are idle shallow things: I am not of your element: you shall know more hereafter.

Exit

MARIA	Nay, pursue him now, lest the device take air and taint.
FABIAN	Why, we shall make him mad indeed.
SIR TOBY BELCH	Come, we'll have him in a dark room and bound. My niece is already in the belief that he's mad: we may carry it thus, for our pleasure and his penance. But see, but see.

Enter SIR ANDREW

FABIAN	More matter for a May morning.
SIR ANDREW	Here's the challenge, read it: warrant there's vinegar and pepper in't.
SIR TOBY BELCH	Give me. *[Reads]*'Youth, whatsoever thou art, thou art but a scurvy fellow.'
FABIAN	Good, and valiant

SIR TOBY BELCH   [Reads] 'Wonder not, nor admire not in thy mind,
why I do call thee so, for I will show thee no reason for't.
Thou comest to the lady Olivia, and in my
sight she uses thee kindly: but thou liest in thy
throat; that is not the matter I challenge thee for.
I will waylay thee going home; where if it
be thy chance to kill me,
Thou killest me like a rogue and a villain.'
Fare thee well; and God have mercy upon
one of our souls! He may have mercy upon mine; but
my hope is better, and so look to thyself. Thy
friend, as thou usest him, and thy sworn enemy,
ANDREW AGUECHEEK.
If this letter move him not, his legs cannot:
I'll give't him.

MARIA   You may have very fit occasion for't: he is now in
some commerce with my lady, and will by and by depart.

SIR TOBY BELCH   Go, Sir Andrew: scout me for him at the corner the
orchard: so soon as ever thou seest
him, draw; and, as thou drawest swear horrible; for
it comes to pass oft that a terrible oath, with a
swaggering accent sharply twanged off, gives manhood
more approbation than ever proof itself would have
earned him. Away!

SIR ANDREW   Nay, let me alone for swearing.
Exit

SIR TOBY BELCH   Now will not I deliver his letter: for the behaviour
of the young gentleman gives him out to be of good
capacity and breeding; his employment between his
lord and my niece confirms no less: therefore this
letter, being so excellently ignorant, will breed no
terror in the youth: he will find it comes from a
clodpole. But, sir, I will deliver his challenge by
word of mouth; set upon Aguecheek a notable report
of valour; and drive the gentleman, as I know his
youth will aptly receive it, into a most hideous

opinion of his rage, skill, fury and impetuosity.
This will so fright them both that they will kill
one another by the look, like cockatrices.

Re-enter OLIVIA, with VIOLA

FABIAN   Here he comes with your niece: give them way till
he take leave, and presently after him.

SIR TOBY BELCH   I will meditate the while upon some horrid message
for a challenge.

Exeunt SIR TOBY BELCH, FABIAN, and MARIA

OLIVIA   I have said too much unto a heart of stone
And laid mine honour too unchary out.

VIOLA   With the same 'haviour that your passion bears
Goes on my master's grief.

OLIVIA   Here, wear this jewel for me, 'tis my picture;
Refuse it not; it hath no tongue to vex you;
And I beseech you come again to-morrow.
What shall you ask of me that I'll deny,
That honour saved may upon asking give?

VIOLA   Nothing but this; your true love for my master.

OLIVIA   How with mine honour may I give him that
Which I have given to you?

VIOLA   I will acquit you.

OLIVIA   Well, come again to-morrow: fare thee well:
A fiend like thee might bear my soul to hell.
Exit

Re-enter SIR TOBY BELCH and FABIAN

SIR TOBY BELCH   Gentleman, God save thee.

VIOLA	And you, sir.
SIR TOBY BELCH	That defence thou hast, betake thee to't: of what nature the wrongs are thou hast done him, I know not; but thy intercepter, full of despite, bloody as the hunter, attends thee at the orchard-end: dismount thy tuck, be yare in thy preparation, for thy assailant is quick, skilful and deadly.
VIOLA	You mistake, sir; I am sure no man hath any quarrel to me: my remembrance is very free and clear from any image of offence done to any man.
SIR TOBY BELCH	You'll find it otherwise, I assure you: therefore, if you hold your life at any price, betake you to your guard; for your opposite hath in him what youth, strength, skill and wrath can furnish man withal.
VIOLA	I pray you, sir, what is he?
SIR TOBY BELCH	He is knight, dubbed with unhatched rapier and on carpet consideration; but he is a devil in private brawl: souls and bodies hath he divorced three; and his incensement at this moment is so implacable, that satisfaction can be none but by pangs of death and sepulchre. Hob, nob, is his word; give't or take't.
VIOLA	I am no fighter. I have heard of some kind of men that put quarrels purposely on others, to taste their valour: belike this is a man of that quirk.
SIR TOBY BELCH	Sir, no; his indignation derives itself out of a very competent injury: therefore, get you on and give him his desire.
VIOLA	I beseech you, do me this courteous office, as to know of the knight what my offence to him is.
SIR TOBY BELCH	I will do so. Signior Fabian, stay you by this gentleman till my return.

Exit

VIOLA	Pray you, sir, do you know of this matter?
FABIAN	I know the knight is incensed against you, even to a mortal arbitrement; but nothing of the circumstance more.
VIOLA	I beseech you, what manner of man is he?
FABIAN	He is, indeed, sir, the most skilful, bloody and fatal opposite that you could possibly have found in any part of Illyria. Will you walk towards him? I will make your peace with him if I can.
VIOLA	I shall be much bound to you for't: I am one that had rather go with sir priest than sir knight: I care not who knows so much of my mettle.

Exeunt

Re-enter SIR TOBY BELCH, with SIR ANDREW

SIR TOBY BELCH	Why, man, he's a very devil; I have not seen such a firago. I had a pass with him, rapier, scabbard and all, and he gives me the stuck in with such a mortal motion, that it is inevitable; and on the answer, he pays you as surely as your feet hit the ground they step on. They say he has been fencer to the Sophy.
SIR ANDREW	Pox on't, I'll not meddle with him.
SIR TOBY BELCH	Ay, but he will not now be pacified: Fabian can scarce hold him yonder.
SIR ANDREW	Plague on't, an I thought he had been valiant and so cunning in fence, I'ld have seen him damned ere I'ld have challenged him. Let him let the matter slip, and I'll give him my horse, grey Capilet.

SIR TOBY BELCH	I'll make the motion: stand here, make a good show on't: this shall end without the perdition of souls. *[Aside]* Marry, I'll ride your horse as well as I ride you.

Re-enter FABIAN and VIOLA

	[To FABIAN] I have his horse to take up the quarrel: I have persuaded him the youth's a devil.
FABIAN	He is as horribly conceited of him; and pants and looks pale, as if a bear were at his heels.
SIR TOBY BELCH	*[To VIOLA]* There's no remedy, sir; he will fight with you for's oath sake: therefore draw, for the supportance of his vow; he protests he will not hurt you.
VIOLA	[Aside] Pray God defend me! A little thing would make me tell them how much I lack of a man.
SIR TOBY BELCH	Come, Sir Andrew, there's no remedy; but he has promised me, as he is a gentleman and a soldier, he will not hurt you. Come on; to't.
SIR ANDREW	Pray God, he keep his oath!
VIOLA	I do assure you, 'tis against my will.

They draw. Enter ANTONIO

ANTONIO	Put up your sword. If this young gentleman Have done offence, I take the fault on me: If you offend him, I for him defy you.
SIR TOBY BELCH	You, sir! why, what are you?
ANTONIO	One, sir, that for his love dares yet do more Than you have heard him brag to you he will.
SIR TOBY BELCH	Nay, if you be an undertaker, I am for you.

49

They draw. Enter Officers

FABIAN	O good Sir Toby, hold! here come the officers.
SIR TOBY BELCH	I'll be with you anon.
VIOLA	Pray, sir, put your sword up, if you please.
SIR ANDREW	Marry, will I, sir; and, for that I promised you, I'll be as good as my word: he will bear you easily and reins well.
First Officer	This is the man; do thy office.
Second Officer	Antonio, I arrest thee at the suit of Count Orsino.
ANTONIO	You do mistake me, sir.
First Officer	No, sir, no jot; I know your favour well, Though now you have no sea-cap on your head. Take him away: he knows I know him well.
ANTONIO	I must obey. *[To VIOLA]* This comes with seeking you: But there's no remedy; I shall answer it. What will you do, now my necessity Makes me to ask you for my purse?
Second Officer	Come, sir, away.
ANTONIO	I must entreat of you some of that money.
VIOLA	What money, sir?
ANTONIO	Will you deny me now? Is't possible that my deserts to you Can lack persuasion? Do not tempt my misery, Lest that it make me so unsound a man As to upbraid you with those kindnesses That I have done for you.

VIOLA	I know of none;
	Nor know I you by voice or any feature.
Second Officer	Come, sir, I pray you, go.
ANTONIO	Let me speak a little. This youth that you see here
	I snatch'd one half out of the jaws of death.
	But O how vile an idol proves this god
	Thou hast, Sebastian, done good feature shame.
First Officer	Come, come, sir.
ANTONIO	Lead me on.
Exit with Officers	
VIOLA	Methinks his words do from such passion fly,
	That he believes himself: so do not I.
	Prove true, imagination, O, prove true,
	That I, dear brother, be now ta'en for you!
	He named Sebastian: O, if it prove,
	Tempests are kind and salt waves fresh in love.
Exit	
SIR TOBY BELCH	A very dishonest paltry boy, leaving his
	friend here in necessity and denying him.
FABIAN	A coward, a most devout coward, religious in it.
SIR ANDREW	'Slid, I'll after him again and beat him.
SIR TOBY BELCH	Do; cuff him soundly, but never draw thy sword.
FABIAN	Come, let's see the event.
Exeunt	

ACT IV

Act IV SCENE I

Before OLIVIA's house

Enter SEBASTIAN and Clown

Clown   Will you make me believe that I am not sent for you?

SEBASTIAN   Go to, go to, thou art a foolish fellow:
Let me be clear of thee.

Clown   Well held out, i' faith! No, I do not know you; nor
I am not sent to you by my lady, to bid you come
speak with her; nor your name is not Master Cesario;
nor this is not my nose neither. Nothing that is so is so.

SEBASTIAN   I prithee, vent thy folly somewhere else: Thou
know'st not me.

Clown   Vent my folly! I prithee tell me what I shall vent to my
lady: shall I vent to her that thou art coming?

SEBASTIAN   I prithee, foolish Greek, depart from me: There's
money for thee: if you tarry longer, I shall give
worse payment.

Enter SIR ANDREW, SIR TOBY BELCH, and FABIAN

SIR ANDREW   Now, sir, have I met you again? there's for you.

SEBASTIAN   Why, there's for thee, and there, and there. Are all
the people mad?

SIR TOBY BELCH Hold, sir, or I'll throw your dagger o'er the house.

Clown   This will I tell my lady straight: I would not be
in some of your coats for two pence.

Exit

SIR TOBY BELCH	Come on, sir; hold.

SIR ANDREW	Nay, let him alone: I'll have an action of battery against him, if there be any law in Illyria: though I struck him first, yet it's no matter for that.

SEBASTIAN	Let go thy hand.

SIR TOBY BELCH	Come, sir, I will not let you go.

SEBASTIAN	If thou darest tempt me further, draw thy sword.

SIR TOBY BELCH	What, what? Nay, then I must have an ounce or two of this malapert blood from you.

Enter OLIVIA

OLIVIA	Hold, Toby; on thy life I charge thee, hold!

SIR TOBY BELCH	Madam!

OLIVIA	Will it be ever thus? Ungracious wretch, out of my sight! Be not offended, dear Cesario. Rudesby, be gone!

Exeunt SIR TOBY BELCH, SIR ANDREW, and FABIAN

	I prithee, gentle friend, Let thy fair wisdom, not thy passion, sway In this uncivil and thou unjust extent Against thy peace. Go with me to my house, And hear thou there how many fruitless pranks This ruffian hath botch'd up, that thou thereby Mayst smile at this: thou shalt not choose but go: Do not deny.

SEBASTIAN	What relish is in this? how runs the stream? Or I am mad, or else this is a dream:

Let fancy still my sense in Lethe steep;
If it be thus to dream, still let me sleep!

OLIVIA   Nay, come, I prithee; would thou'ldst be ruled by me!

SEBASTIAN   Madam, I will.

OLIVIA   O, say so, and so be!

Exeunt

Act IV Scene II

OLIVIA's house

Enter MARIA and Clown

MARIA　　　　　　Nay, I prithee, put on this gown and this beard;
make him believe thou art Sir Topas the curate: do
it quickly; I'll call Sir Toby the whilst.

Exit MARIA. Enter SIR TOBY BELCH

SIR TOBY BELCH　Jove bless thee, master Parson.

Clown　　　　　　Bonos dies, Sir Toby.

SIR TOBY BELCH　To him, Sir Topas.

Clown　　　　　　What, ho, I say! peace in this prison!

MALVOLIO　　　　[Within] Who calls there?

Clown　　　　　　Sir Topas the curate, who comes to visit Malvolio
the lunatic.

MALVOLIO　　　　Sir Topas, Sir Topas, good Sir Topas, go to my lady.

Clown　　　　　　Out, hyperbolical fiend! how vexest thou this man!
talkest thou nothing but of ladies?

MALVOLIO　　　　Sir Topas, never was man thus wronged: good Sir
Topas, do not think I am mad: they have laid me
here in hideous darkness.

Clown　　　　　　Fie, thou dishonest Satan! sayest thou that house is dark?

MALVOLIO　　　　As hell, Sir Topas.

Clown	Why it hath bay windows transparent as barricadoes, and yet complainest thou of obstruction?
MALVOLIO	I am not mad, Sir Topas: I say to you, this house is dark.
Clown	Madman, thou errest: I say, there is no darkness.
MALVOLIO	I say, this house is as dark as ignorance, though ignorance were as dark as hell; and I say, there was never man thus abused. I am no more mad than you.
Clown	Fare thee well. Remain thou still in darkness.
MALVOLIO	Sir Topas, Sir Topas!
Clown	Nay, I am for all waters.
SIR TOBY BELCH	To him in thine own voice, and bring me word how thou findest him: I would we were well rid of this knavery for I am now so far in offence with my niece that I cannot pursue with any safety this sport to the upshot. Come by and by to my chamber.

Exeunt SIR TOBY BELCH and MARIA

Clown	[Singing] 'Hey, Robin, jolly Robin, Tell me how thy lady does.'
MALVOLIO	Fool!
Clown	Who calls, ha? Master Malvolio?
MALVOLIO	Ay, good fool.
Clown	Alas, sir, how fell you besides your five wits?
MALVOLIO	Fool, there was never a man so notoriously abused. They have here propertied me; keep me in darkness, send ministers to me, asses, and do all they can to face me out of my wits. Good fool, some ink, paper and light; and convey what I will set down to my lady:

	it shall advantage thee more than ever the bearing of letter did.
Clown	I will help you to't. But tell me true, are you not mad indeed? or do you but counterfeit?
MALVOLIO	Believe me, I am not; I tell thee true.
Clown	Nay, I'll ne'er believe a madman till I see his brains. I will fetch you light and paper and ink.

Exit

Act IV Scene III

OLIVIA's garden

Enter SEBASTIAN

SEBASTIAN   This is the air; that is the glorious sun;
This pearl she gave me, I do feel't and see't;
And though 'tis wonder that enwraps me thus,
Yet 'tis not madness. Where's Antonio, then?
I could not find him at the Elephant:
His counsel now might do me golden service.
For though this accident and flood of fortune
So far exceed all instance, all discourse,
That I am ready to distrust mine eyes
And wrangle with my reason that persuades me
To any other trust but that I am mad
Or else the lady's mad; But here the lady comes.

Enter OLIVIA and Priest

OLIVIA   Blame not this haste of mine. If you mean well,
Now go with me and with this holy man
Into the chantry by: there, before him,
And underneath that consecrated roof,
Plight me the full assurance of your faith;
That my most jealous and too doubtful soul
May live at peace. He shall conceal it
Whiles you are willing it shall come to note,
What time we will our celebration keep
According to my birth. What do you say?

SEBASTIAN   I'll follow this good man, and go with you;
And, having sworn truth, ever will be true.

OLIVIA   Then lead the way, good father; and heavens so shine,
That they may fairly note this act of mine!

Exeunt

ACT V

Act V Scene I

Before OLIVIA's house

Enter Clown and FABIAN Enter DUKE ORSINO, VIOLA, CURIO, and Lords

DUKE ORSINO   Belong you to the Lady Olivia, friends?

Clown   Ay, sir; we are some of her trappings.

DUKE ORSINO   If you will let your lady know I am here to speak
with her, and bring her along with you, it may awake
my bounty further.

Clown   Marry, sir, lullaby to your bounty till I come
again.

Exit

VIOLA   Here comes the man, sir, that did rescue me.

Enter ANTONIO and Officers

DUKE ORSINO   That face of his I do remember well;
Yet, when I saw it last, it was besmear'd
As black as Vulcan in the smoke of war:
A bawbling vessel was he captain of,
For shallow draught and bulk unprizable;
With which such scathful grapple did he make
With the most noble bottom of our fleet,
That very envy and the tongue of loss
Cried fame and honour on him. What's the matter?

First Officer   Orsino, this is that Antonio
That took the Phoenix and her fraught from Candy;
And this is he that did the Tiger board,
When your young nephew Titus lost his leg:

Here in the streets, desperate of shame and state,
In private brabble did we apprehend him.

VIOLA

He did me kindness, sir, drew on my side;
But in conclusion put strange speech upon me:
I know not what 'twas but distraction.

DUKE ORSINO

Notable pirate! thou salt-water thief!
What foolish boldness brought thee to their mercies,
Whom thou, in terms so bloody and so dear,
Hast made thine enemies?

ANTONIO

Orsino, noble sir,
Be pleased that I shake off these names you give me:
Antonio never yet was thief or pirate,
Though I confess, on base and ground enough,
Orsino's enemy. A witchcraft drew me hither:
That most ingrateful boy there by your side,
From the rude sea's enraged and foamy mouth
Did I redeem; a wreck past hope he was:
His life I gave him and did thereto add
My love, without retention or restraint,
All his in dedication; for his sake
Did I expose myself, pure for his love,
Into the danger of this adverse town;
Drew to defend him when he was beset:
Where being apprehended, his false cunning,
Not meaning to partake with me in danger,
Taught him to face me out of his acquaintance,
denied me mine own purse,
Which I had recommended to his use
Not half an hour before.

VIOLA

How can this be?

DUKE ORSINO

When came he to this town?

ANTONIO

To-day, my lord; and for three months before,
No interim, not a minute's vacancy,
Both day and night did we keep company.

Enter OLIVIA and Attendants

DUKE ORSINO   Here comes the countess: now heaven walks on earth.
But for thee, fellow; fellow, thy words are madness:
Three months this youth hath tended upon me;
But more of that anon. Take him aside.

OLIVIA   What would my lord, but that he may not have,
Wherein Olivia may seem serviceable?
Cesario, you do not keep promise with me.

VIOLA   Madam!

DUKE ORSINO   Gracious Olivia,--

OLIVIA   What do you say, Cesario? Good my lord,--

VIOLA   My lord would speak; my duty hushes me.

OLIVIA   If it be aught to the old tune, my lord,
It is as fat and fulsome to mine ear
As howling after music.

DUKE ORSINO   Still so cruel?

OLIVIA   Still so constant, lord.

DUKE ORSINO   What, to perverseness? you uncivil lady,
To whose ingrate and unauspicious altars
My soul the faithfull'st offerings hath breathed out
That e'er devotion tender'd! What shall I do?

OLIVIA   Even what it please my lord, that shall become him.

DUKE ORSINO   Why should I not, had I the heart to do it,
Kill what I love? But hear me:
This your minion, whom I know you love,
And whom, by heaven I swear, I tender dearly,
Him will I tear out of that cruel eye,
Where he sits crowned in his master's spite.

	Come, boy, with me; my thoughts are ripe in mischief: I'll sacrifice the lamb that I do love, To spite a raven's heart within a dove.
VIOLA	And I, most jocund, apt and willingly, To do you rest, a thousand deaths would die.
OLIVIA	Where goes Cesario?
VIOLA	After him I love More than I love these eyes, more than my life, More, by all mores, than e'er I shall love wife.
OLIVIA	Ay me, detested! how am I beguiled!
VIOLA	Who does beguile you? who does do you wrong?
OLIVIA	Hast thou forgot thyself? is it so long? Call forth the holy father.
DUKE ORSINO	Come, away!
OLIVIA	Whither, my lord? Cesario, husband, stay.
DUKE ORSINO	Husband!
OLIVIA	Ay, husband: can he that deny?
DUKE ORSINO	Her husband, sirrah!
VIOLA	No, my lord, not I.
OLIVIA	Alas, it is the baseness of thy fear That makes thee strangle thy propriety: Fear not, Cesario; take thy fortunes up; Be that thou know'st thou art, and then thou art As great as that thou fear'st.

Enter Priest

O, welcome, father!
Father, I charge thee, by thy reverence,
Here to unfold, what thou dost know
Hath newly pass'd between this youth and me.

Priest

A contract of eternal bond of love,
Confirm'd by mutual joinder of your hands,
Attested by the holy close of lips,
Strengthen'd by interchangement of your rings;
And all the ceremony of this compact
Seal'd in my function, by my testimony:
Since when, my watch hath told me, toward my grave
I have travell'd but two hours.

DUKE ORSINO

O thou dissembling cub!
Farewell, and take her; but direct thy feet
Where thou and I henceforth may never meet.

VIOLA

My lord, I do protest--

OLIVIA

O, do not swear!
Hold little faith, though thou hast too much fear.

Enter SIR ANDREW

SIR ANDREW

For the love of God, a surgeon! Send one presently
to Sir Toby.

OLIVIA

What's the matter?

SIR ANDREW

He has broke my head across and has given Sir Toby
a bloody coxcomb too: for the love of God, your
help!

OLIVIA

Who has done this, Sir Andrew?

SIR ANDREW

The count's gentleman, one Cesario: we took him for
a coward, but he's the very devil incardinate.

DUKE ORSINO

My gentleman, Cesario?

SIR ANDREW	'Od's lifelings, here he is! You broke my head for nothing; and that that I did, I was set on to do't by Sir Toby.
VIOLA	Why do you speak to me? I never hurt you: You drew your sword upon me without cause; But I bespoke you fair, and hurt you not.

Enter SIR TOBY BELCH and Clown

DUKE ORSINO	How now, gentleman! how is't with you?
SIR TOBY BELCH	That's all one: has hurt me, and there's the end on't. Sot, didst see Dick surgeon, sot?
OLIVIA	Get him to bed, and let his hurt be look'd to.

Exeunt Clown, FABIAN, SIR TOBY BELCH, and SIR ANDREW

Enter SEBASTIAN

SEBASTIAN	I am sorry, madam, I have hurt your kinsman: But, had it been the brother of my blood, I must have done no less with wit and safety. You throw a strange regard upon me, and by that I do perceive it hath offended you: Pardon me, sweet one, even for the vows We made each other but so late ago.
DUKE ORSINO	One face, one voice, one habit, and two persons, A natural perspective, that is and is not!
SEBASTIAN	Antonio, O my dear Antonio! How have the hours rack'd and tortured me, Since I have lost thee!
ANTONIO	Sebastian are you?
SEBASTIAN	Fear'st thou that, Antonio?

ANTONIO	How have you made division of yourself?
	An apple, cleft in two, is not more twin
	Than these two creatures. Which is Sebastian?
OLIVIA	Most wonderful!
SEBASTIAN	Do I stand there? I never had a brother;
	Nor can there be that deity in my nature,
	Of here and every where. I had a sister,
	Whom the blind waves and surges have devour'd.
	Of charity, what kin are you to me?
	What countryman? what name? what parentage?
VIOLA	Of Messaline: Sebastian was my father;
	Such a Sebastian was my brother too,
	So went he suited to his watery tomb:
	If spirits can assume both form and suit
	You come to fright us.
SEBASTIAN	A spirit I am indeed;
	But am in that dimension grossly clad
	Which from the womb I did participate.
	Were you a woman, as the rest goes even,
	I should my tears let fall upon your cheek,
	And say 'Thrice-welcome, drowned Viola!'
VIOLA	My father had a mole upon his brow.
SEBASTIAN	And so had mine.
VIOLA	And died that day when Viola from her birth
	Had number'd thirteen years.
SEBASTIAN	O, that record is lively in my soul!
	He finished indeed his mortal act
	That day that made my sister thirteen years.
VIOLA	If nothing lets to make us happy both
	But this my masculine usurp'd attire,
	Do not embrace me till each circumstance

Of place, time, fortune, do cohere and jump
That I am Viola.

SEBASTIAN   [To OLIVIA] So comes it, lady, you have been mistook:
                   But nature to her bias drew in that.
                   You would have been contracted to a maid;
                   Nor are you therein, by my life, deceived,
                   You are betroth'd both to a maid and man.

DUKE ORSINO   Be not amazed; right noble is his blood.
                   If this be so, as yet the glass seems true,
                   I shall have share in this most happy wreck.
                   [To VIOLA] Boy, thou hast said to me a thousand times
                   Thou never shouldst love woman like to me.

VIOLA   And all those sayings will I overswear;
                   And those swearings keep as true in soul
                   As doth that orbed continent the fire
                   That severs day from night.

DUKE ORSINO   Give me thy hand;
                   And let me see thee in thy woman's weeds.

VIOLA   The captain that did bring me first on shore
                   Hath my maid's garments: he upon some action
                   Is now in durance, at Malvolio's suit,
                   A gentleman, and follower of my lady's.

OLIVIA   He shall enlarge him: fetch Malvolio hither:
                   And yet, alas, now I remember me,
                   They say, poor gentleman, he's much distract.

Re-enter Clown with a letter, and FABIAN

                   A most extracting frenzy of mine own
                   From my remembrance clearly banish'd his.
                   How does he, sirrah?

Clown   Truly, madam, he has here writ a letter to you.

OLIVIA	*[To FABIAN]* Open't, and read it you, sirrah.
FABIAN	[Reads] 'By the Lord, madam, you wrong me, and the world shall know it: though you have put me into darkness and given your drunken cousin rule over me, yet have I the benefit of my senses as well as your ladyship. I have your own letter that induced me to the semblance I put on; with the which I doubt not but to do myself much right, or you much shame. Think of me as you please. I leave my duty a little unthought of and speak out of my injury. THE MADLY-USED MALVOLIO.'
OLIVIA	Did he write this?
Clown	Ay, madam.
DUKE ORSINO	This savours not much of distraction.
OLIVIA	Fabian; bring him hither.

Exit FABIAN

> My lord so please you, these things further thought on,
> To think me as well a sister as a wife,
> One day shall crown the alliance on't, so please you,
> Here at my house and at my proper cost.

DUKE ORSINO	Madam, I am most apt to embrace your offer. *[To VIOLA]* Your master quits you; and for your service done him, So much against the mettle of your sex, So far beneath your soft and tender breeding, And since you call'd me master for so long, Here is my hand: you shall from this time be Your master's mistress.
OLIVIA	A sister! you are she.

Re-enter FABIAN, with MALVOLIO

DUKE ORSINO	Is this the madman?
OLIVIA	Ay, my lord, this same. How now, Malvolio!
MALVOLIO	Madam, you have done me wrong, Notorious wrong.
OLIVIA	Have I, Malvolio? no.
MALVOLIO	Lady, you have. Pray you, peruse that letter. You must not now deny it is your hand: Or say 'tis not your seal, nor your invention: You can say none of this.
OLIVIA	Alas, Malvolio, this is not my writing, But out of question 'tis Maria's hand. Prithee, be content: But when we know the grounds and authors of it, Thou shalt be both the plaintiff and the judge Of thine own cause.
FABIAN	Good madam, most freely I confess, myself and Toby Set this device against Malvolio here, Upon some stubborn and uncourteous parts We had conceived against him: Maria writ The letter at Sir Toby's great importance; In recompense whereof he hath married her.
OLIVIA	Alas, poor fool, how have they baffled thee!
Clown	Why, 'some are born great, some achieve greatness, and some have greatness thrown upon them.' I was one, sir, in this interlude; one Sir Topas, sir; but that's all one. 'By the Lord, fool, I am not mad.' But do you remember? 'Madam, why laugh you at such a barren rascal? an you smile not, he's gagged:' and thus the whirligig of time brings in his revenges.
MALVOLIO *Exit*	I'll be revenged on the whole pack of you.

OLIVIA   He hath been most notoriously abused.

DUKE ORSINO   Pursue him and entreat him to a peace:
                    He hath not told us of the captain yet:
                    When that is known and golden time convents,
                    A solemn combination shall be made
                    Of our dear souls. Meantime, sweet sister,
                    We will not part from hence. Cesario, come;
                    For so you shall be, while you are a man;
                    But when in other habits you are seen,
                    Orsino's mistress and his fancy's queen.

Exeunt all

Other Abridged Shakespeare Plays in the Series

CPSIA information can be obtained
at www.ICGtesting.com
Printed in the USA
LVHW080955191222
735524LV00021B/322